My Favorite RECIP

I love cooking and all the things that go with it—choosing ingredients, learning new skills, having fun with friends in the kitchen, and making delicious recipes. In this new flip-over book, I've chosen a selection of my very favorite recipes for you to try at home. There are savory and sweet dishes, so whatever you like to eat, there is something here for you. Happy cooking!

ANNABEL KARMEL

A collection of your favorite recipes previously published in *Mom and Me Cookbook*, *The Toddler Cookbook*, *Cook It Together*, and *You Can Cook*

DK Publishing

LONDON, NEW YORK, MUNICH,
MELBOURNE, and DELHI

Senior Editor Penny Smith
Senior Designer Rachael Grady

DK India
Editor Garima Sharma
Senior Designer Neha Ahuja
Managing Editor Glenda Fernandes
Managing Art Editor Romi Chakroborty
DTP Manager Sunil Sharma
DTP Operator Sourabh Challariya

Photographer Dave King
Production Editor Siu Yin Chan
Production Controller Claire Pearson
Jacket Editor Matilda Gollon
Jacket Designer Rachael Grady
Publishing Manager Bridget Giles
Art Director Martin Wilson
Creative Director Jane Bull
Category Publisher Mary Ling
US Editors Liza Kaplan, Margaret Parrish

For my children Nicholas, Lara, and Scarlett
First American edition, 2011

Recipes compiled from Annabel Karmel's *Mom and Me Cookbook*,
The Toddler Cookbook, *Cook It Together*, and *You Can Cook*

First published in the United States by DK Publishing
375 Hudson Street, New York, New York 10014

11 12 13 14 15 10 9 8 7 6 5 4 3 2 1
180028—November 2010

Copyright © 2011 Dorling Kindersley Limited
A Penguin Company

A catalog record for this book
is available from the Library of Congress.
ISBN: 978-0-7566-7195-2

Color reproduction by Media Development and Printing Ltd, UK
Printed and bound by Hung Hing, China

www.dk.com

Annabel Karmel

Annabel Karmel is a best-selling
author on cooking for children and her
books are published all over the world.

She is an expert in devising tasty and
nutritious meals for children without
the need to spend hours in the kitchen.

Annabel writes for many newspapers and magazines and
appears frequently on radio and TV as one of the
UK's experts on children's nutritional needs. She has her
own range of healthy foods for children in supermarkets
and a co-branded line of children's foods with Disney. She
also produces a range of kids' cooking equipment.

Annabel was awarded an MBE in the 2006 Queen's
Honours List for her outstanding work in the field of
child nutrition.

Visit Annabel's website at
www.annabelkarmel.com

annabel karmel

⚠ Take care!

All the recipes in this book are to be made under
adult supervision. However, when this symbol
appears, extra care should be taken.

Acknowledgments

With thanks from Annabel to: Caroline Stearns,
Seiko Hatfield, Dave King, Mary Ling, Penny Smith,
Evelyn Etkind, and Liz Beckett.

All images © Dorling Kindersley
For further information see: www.dkimages.com

Contents

How to make tomato soup

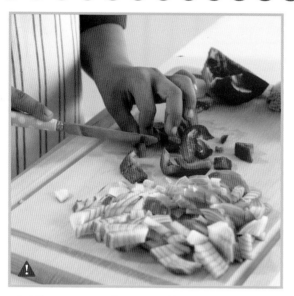

1 First, prepare the vegetables: chop the onion and dice the pepper.

2 Peel the carrot, then shred it on the roughest side of the grater. Crush the garlic.

Simmer for 30 minutes.

3 Heat the oil, and add the onion, pepper, and carrot. Cook for 5 minutes. Add the canned tomatoes, tomato paste, ketchup, garlic, sugar, thyme, and broth.

4 Season the mixture with salt and pepper. Then blend the soup until it's smooth. Stir in the heavy cream and serve.

Tomato soup

This is tomato soup with a smile. It makes a delicious light meal when served with crispy bread or breadsticks.

You will need:

1 small red onion
½ small red bell pepper
½ carrot
1 clove garlic
1 tbsp olive oil
14 oz (400 g) can diced
   tomatoes
3 tbsp tomato paste
3 tbsp ketchup
2 tbsp superfine sugar
1 sprig fresh thyme leaves
   (about 10 leaves)
1 cup vegetable broth
salt and pepper
¼ cup heavy cream
basil leaves, olive slices,
   cream, to serve

☆ Annabel's Tip

To decorate your soup with funny faces, make eyes from basil leaves and slices of olive, then pipe on the rest of the faces using cream. Remember, the cooler the soup, the longer your faces will stay put!

How to make corn chowder

🥄 PREPARATION TIME **15 minutes**   🕐 COOKING TIME **about 45 minutes**   🍽 SERVES 6

1 Chop the onion, crush the garlic, and peel and cut the potatoes into small cubes.

2 Melt the butter in a large saucepan. Cook the onion and garlic very gently for 10 to 12 minutes.

3 Add the potato cubes, broth, and milk. Bring the mixture to a boil, then reduce the heat and simmer, partly covered, for 15 minutes.

4 Add the corn and simmer (partly covered) for 10 minutes, or until the potato is soft. If the mixture feels very thick, add 2 tbsp hot water.

5 Let the mixture cool, then put half aside. Blend the remaining soup in the pan. Then add the saved soup, heat, and serve with cream on top.

Corn chowder

A chowder is a lusciously thick and warming soup, usually made with potato. Here is a vegetarian recipe, but you can make a chicken version by adding cooked chicken at step 5, and using chicken broth.

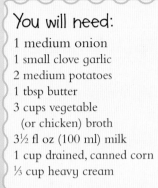

You will need:

1 medium onion
1 small clove garlic
2 medium potatoes
1 tbsp butter
3 cups vegetable
 (or chicken) broth
3½ fl oz (100 ml) milk
1 cup drained, canned corn
⅓ cup heavy cream

Sprinkle with dill weed

Serve with crusty bread

☆Annabel's Tip

For chicken chowder, add ⅔ cup shredded, cooked chicken at step 5.

How to make a basic egg omelet

1 Break the eggs into a bowl and whisk them until they are slightly frothy. Season with salt and pepper.

2 Heat a small frying pan—about 7 in (17 cm)—over medium heat. Melt the butter and when it starts to foam, pour in the eggs.

3 Stir the eggs lightly once or twice, then leave them to cook undisturbed for about 30 seconds.

4 When the eggs start to set at the edges, lift the cooked edge toward the center and tip the pan so the uncooked egg runs into the empty space.

5 Now add the filling of your choice. Turn off the heat and fold the omelet over. Transfer it to a plate and serve immediately.

Basic egg omelet

Here's how you make a delicious basic omelet. Serve it plain, try one of my filling suggestions (right), or invent your own!

☆ Annabel's Tip

If you are adding herbs to your omelet, either sprinkle them on the cooked omelet, or stir into the raw eggs at step 1.

You will need:

2 eggs
salt and pepper
2 tsp butter

Omelet fillings

- 1 oz (30 g) ham, cut into strips, with slices of tomato
- ¼ cup grated hard cheese such as Cheddar or Gruyére
- 1 oz (30 g) smoked salmon, cut into thin strips
- 1 tsp chopped soft herbs—try parsley with dill weed, chervil, or chives
- 1 tbsp each corn and diced red bell pepper, plus one thinly sliced scallion
- a handful of button mushrooms sautéed in 2 tsp of butter

How to make avocado dip

🥑 PREPARATION TIME **10 minutes**   🍴 SERVES **2-4**

1 Cut the avocado in half, remove the pit, and scoop out the flesh.

2 Squeeze lemon juice onto the avocado flesh to help it keep its color.

3 Mash up the avocado and lemon juice and mix it with the sour cream.

4 Chop the tomato into tiny pieces. Add to the avocado along with the chives.

5 Season with salt and pepper and mix everything together. Serve with vegetables and strips of pita bread.

Avocado frog dip

This avocado and tomato dip is perfect for all ages—but give it a face and younger children won't be able to resist it!

☆ Annabel's Tip

Make a frog face using cucumber and olives for eyes and chives for a mouth.

You will need:

1 large avocado
1 tbsp lemon juice
2 tbsp sour cream
1 tomato
1½ tsp snipped chives
salt and pepper
cucumber, carrots, red bell pepper, and pita bread, to serve

Carrot sticks

Strips of pita bread

Cucumber sticks

Red bell pepper slices

How to make chicken dippers

1 Mix the ingredients for the marinade in a large bowl. Coat the chicken slices in the marinade. Cover and leave for at least an hour.

2 Next, preheat the oven to 400°F (200°C). Crush the potato chips into crumbs in a plastic bag. Then mix them with the Parmesan cheese.

3 Mix the flour and pepper in one bowl. Beat the egg with 1 tbsp cold water in a separate bowl. Dip the chicken in the flour, egg, and then the crumbs.

4 When done, place the chicken strips onto a baking sheet. Bake in the oven for 15 minutes.

Turn over after 7 minutes.

5 Mix the ingredients for each sauce in a small bowl, ready to dip your cooked crunchy chicken in.

Chicken dippers

These strips of chicken are coated in potato chips! I've used cheese-flavored chips, but you can choose whatever flavor you like best. Serve with my quick-and-easy dips.

You will need:

9 oz (250 g) chicken breast, cut into thin slices
5 oz (150 g) bag good-quality cheese-flavored potato chips
5 tbsp grated Parmesan cheese
⅓ cup all-purpose flour
pepper
1 egg

For the marinade
1 cup buttermilk
1 tsp Worcestershire sauce
1 tsp soy sauce
1 small clove garlic, crushed
¼ tsp paprika
¼ tsp dried oregano

Maple mustard mayo

¼ cup mayonnaise
1 tsp wholegrain Dijon mustard
1½ tsp maple syrup or honey
1 tsp cold water

Slightly spicy tomato

½ tsp Thai sweet chili sauce
2 tbsp ketchup
2 tsp lime juice

How to make easy cheesy bread rolls

PREPARATION **30 minutes, plus rising**   COOKING TIME **12–14 minutes**   MAKES **8-16 rolls**

1 Put the yeast, sugar, and 3 tbsp water in a bowl. Stir to dissolve the yeast. Let stand for 5 minutes, or until frothy.

2 Meanwhile, grate the Cheddar cheese using the large grater holes, and the Parmesan using the fine holes.

3 Stir the flour and salt together in a large bowl. Make a dip in the center and add the oil and the yeast liquid.

4 Add the rest of the water and mix to a soft dough. Add a teaspoon of extra water if the dough is dry.

5 Turn onto a floured surface and knead until smooth—this will take about 10 minutes.

6 Pat the dough into a circle about 8 in (20 cm) across. Spread the grated cheese over it, then fold the dough in half.

7 Fold in half again, so the cheese is enclosed. Knead for 1-2 minutes more. Then divide into about 8 pieces.

8 Shape the dough into balls and place on an oiled baking sheet. Leave to rise for 45 minutes, or until doubled in size.

Bake for 12–14 minutes.

9 Preheat the oven to 400°F (200°C). Brush the dough with the beaten egg. Sprinkle with seeds and bake.

Easy cheesy bread rolls

There is nothing like the taste of fresh bread!
These cheesy rolls are perfect for packed
lunches or a picnic treat.

You will need:

1 x ¼ oz (7 g) envelope of
active dry yeast

1 tsp sugar

⅔ cup hand-hot water

2 oz (60 g) mature Cheddar
cheese

1 oz (30 g) Parmesan cheese

2 cups white bread flour,
plus extra for dusting

¼ tsp salt

1 tbsp canola oil, plus extra
for greasing

1 egg, beaten with a pinch of
salt

sesame, sunflower, pumpkin,
and poppy seeds, for sprinkling

How to knead dough

*Use the heel of your hand to
squash the dough away from
you. Then fold the top end over
toward you and turn the
dough a quarter turn clockwise.
Repeat this until the dough is
smooth and silky.*

Tomato bruschetta

Bruschetta is Italian for toast, and these warm, juicy tomatoes on toast make a lovely lunch or light dinner.

You will need:

9 oz (250 g) cherry or grape
  tomatoes (about 20)
1 tbsp olive oil
4 small sprigs of thyme
salt and pepper
4 slices country-style bread
1 clove garlic, halved
small bunch basil leaves
1 oz (30 g) Parmesan cheese

☆Annabel's Tip

*For big flakes of Parmesan,
shave slices off a block
of cheese using a
vegetable peeler.*

🍲 PREPARATION TIME **10 minutes**   🕐 COOKING TIME **about 10 minutes**   🍽 SERVES **2-4**

1 Preheat the oven to 400°F (200°C). Line a baking sheet with parchment paper. Halve the tomatoes and sit them on this.

2 Drizzle 1 tsp of the olive oil over the top. Scatter over the thyme leaves. Season with salt and pepper. Bake the tomatoes for 6-8 minutes, or until soft.

3 Toast the bread. Rub the garlic over one side of the toast. Trickle the remaining olive oil on top. Top with the baked tomatoes, basil, and Parmesan.

Cobb salad

An American invention, this tasty salad is made with avocado, hard-boiled eggs, and chicken. Serve it with fresh crusty bread for a meal.

You will need:

2 eggs
2 oz (60 g) Cheddar cheese
2 oz (60 g) skinless chicken
  breast, cooked
1 large tomato
1 small avocado
1 small heart romaine lettuce

For the dressing
3 tbsp mayonnaise
3 tbsp milk
½ tsp red wine vinegar
¼ tsp Dijon mustard
2-3 drops Worcestershire sauce
salt and pepper

☆ Annabel's Tip
To make the dressing, mix together the dressing ingredients and serve with the salad.

PREPARATION TIME **20 minutes**   COOKING TIME **12 minutes**   SERVES 2

1 Bring a saucepan of water to a boil. Lower the eggs into the water and simmer for 12 minutes. Then cool under cold running water.

2 Peel the eggs and cut each one into four lengthwise. Dice the cheese and chicken into very small cubes. Cut the tomato into eight.

3 Slice the avocado and remove the skin. Then arrange the lettuce, avocado, egg, tomato, chicken, and cheese in a bowl.

How to make Caesar salad

PREPARATION TIME **15 minutes**   COOKING TIME **9 minutes**   SERVES **2-4**

Toast each side for 2 minutes.

Toast for 4-5 minutes.

1 For the croutons, cut star and heart shapes out of the bread using mini cookie cutters. Toast under the broiler.

2 Sprinkle 2 tbsp of the grated Parmesan over the toasted croutons and toast again.

3 To make the dressing, mix together the garlic, lemon juice, mayonnaise, Worcestershire sauce, water, and remaining Parmesan.

Mix together

4 Season the dressing with salt and pepper. Then add the lettuce leaves (tear the bigger ones into smaller pieces).

5 Mix together the lettuce and dressing. Scatter the croutons on top and serve.

Caesar salad

This lettuce salad has a delicious dressing— and such lovely cheesy croutons that you may want to make extra to serve with soup.

You will need:

For the croutons
2–3 slices white bread
2 tbsp grated Parmesan cheese

For the dressing
½ small clove garlic, crushed
¼ tsp lemon juice
⅓ cup mayonnaise
4–5 drops Worcestershire sauce
2 tbsp cold water
2 tbsp grated Parmesan cheese
salt and pepper

For the salad
2 hearts of romaine lettuce

Try it...

... with chicken
Marinate 2 chicken breasts for 1 hour in olive oil, a little lemon juice, and 1 crushed clove of garlic. Broil the chicken. Slice and scatter over the salad.

How to make corn fritters

🥣 PREPARATION TIME **20 minutes**   🕐 COOKING TIME **12 minutes**   🍴 MAKES **8-10 fritters**

1 Separate the egg by tipping the yolk from one half of the shell to the other. Let the egg white fall into one bowl and drop the yolk into another.

2 Whisk the egg yolk with the maple syrup and milk. Sift the flour, baking powder, and salt into a bowl. Pour in the egg mixture. Whisk into a batter.

3 Then whisk the egg white until it forms stiff peaks. Be careful not to overwhisk or it will go flat.

Mix using a spatula.

4 Carefully fold the egg white, corn, and scallions into the batter.

5 Heat the oil, drop in 2 tbsp batter per fritter, and cook for 1–2 minutes, until golden underneath. Flip over, cook the other side, then serve.

Corn fritters

These lovely golden fritters taste as good as they look! They are popular in the South and are great when eaten with friends and family. For big parties, simply double the quantities!

You will need:

1 egg
1 tbsp maple syrup
2 tbsp milk
1¼ cups all-purpose flour
1 tsp baking powder
pinch of salt
1 cup drained, canned corn
2 scallions, chopped
1-2 tbsp canola oil

☆**Annabel's Tip**
Try dishing up these fritters for an unusual breakfast. Serve them with chopped banana and extra maple syrup.

Serve with tomato and basil ·······

Potato wedges

These wedges are a healthy and an easy alternative to fries, but just as delicious. You can make them spicy by adding paprika or fajita seasoning.

Sour cream dip

You will need:

2 large potatoes
1 tbsp olive oil
salt and pepper
½ tsp paprika or fajita
seasoning (optional)

Sour cream dip

Mix 3 tbsp sour cream, 1 tbsp mayonnaise, 2 tsp milk, 2 tsp snipped chives, ½ crushed clove garlic, and salt and pepper. Serve with the wedges.

PREPARATION TIME **10 minutes**   COOKING TIME **30 minutes**   SERVES 2–4

1 First, preheat the oven to 400°F (200°C). Then cut each potato lengthwise into thick wedges.

2 Put the oil and salt and pepper into a bowl. Add the paprika or fajita seasoning, if using. Then add the potatoes and mix thoroughly.

3 Lay the wedges on a baking sheet lined with parchment paper. Bake for 30 minutes, turning 2 or 3 times, until golden and cooked through.

Roasted parsnip chips

Very simple to make, these crispy and sweet parsnip chips will be a great hit when you have friends over.

You will need:

2 parsnips
2-3 tbsp olive oil
salt and pepper

PREPARATION TIME 15 minutes   **COOKING TIME** 30-35 minutes   SERVES 2-4

1 Preheat the oven to 350°F (180°C). Peel the parsnips and cut off the ends. Then cut the parsnips into thin slices—try and make them all about the same size.

2 Lay the parsnips on a baking sheet lined with parchment paper. Sprinkle with olive oil, and season with salt and pepper. Roast for about 30 minutes, turning every 10-12 minutes, until golden.

How to make chicken pitas

1 Mix together the yogurt, curry paste, honey, and lemon juice in a bowl. Add the chicken and mix to coat. Cover and leave to marinate for 30 minutes (or overnight in the refrigerator).

2 Meanwhile, make the dressing: put the yogurt, lemon juice, and salt into a bowl. Snip the mint into strips. Mix well and keep in the refrigerator until needed.

Broil each side for 6 minutes.

3 Preheat the broiler to low. Put the chicken on a lined baking sheet. Spoon over half the marinade left in the bowl and broil. Flip sides, add the remaining marinade, and broil again.

4 Broil the pitas so they puff up. When cool enough to handle, split them open and fill with the lettuce leaves, chicken, and yogurt dressing. Then serve.

Chicken pitas

This is a mildly spicy dish with a lovely cooling minty dressing. Serve in pita breads for a light lunch or dinner.

Serve while the chicken is still warm

You will need:

For the chicken
¼ cup plain yogurt
1 tsp mild curry paste
1 tsp honey
1 tsp lemon juice
8 chicken mini fillets

For the dressing
¼ cup plain yogurt
1 tsp lemon juice
pinch of salt
8 mint leaves

To serve
4 small pita breads
1 small heart romaine lettuce

☆ Annabel's Tip
Make sure you wash your hands after handling raw chicken. And check that it is cooked all the way through before serving.

How to make rice arancini

1 Heat the oil and cook the onion for 5 minutes. Add the rice and the broth. Simmer for 25 minutes, stirring often. Add 2 tbsp Parmesan, salt, and pepper.

2 Spread the rice out on a plate to cool. Then refrigerate it for 3 hours, or until firm. Break it up, divide it into 5 portions, and form into balls.

3 Make a hole in each ball and push in a piece of mozzarella. Press the rice around the cheese to close up the ball.

4 Mix the bread crumbs with the remaining Parmesan. Dip the rice balls in the egg.

5 Roll the rice balls in the bread crumb mixture. When the balls are completely coated, fry them in oil for 5 minutes, or until golden brown.

Rice arancini

These rice balls with melted cheese centers are delicious. Serve with a ready-made tomato sauce or make your own (see below).

You will need:

1 tsp olive oil
1 tbsp diced onion
¼ cup risotto rice
1 cup chicken or
  vegetable broth
3 tbsp grated Parmesan cheese
salt and pepper
5 oz (150 g) mozzarella, cut
  into 5 x ¾ in (2 cm) pieces
2 tbsp dried bread crumbs
1 egg, beaten with a pinch
  of salt
oil, for frying

Tomato sauce

Heat 1 tbsp olive oil and cook 1 diced shallot and 1 crushed clove of garlic. Add a 14 oz (400 g) can diced tomatoes, 1 tsp brown sugar, and 1 tbsp ketchup. Cook for 15 minutes.

......*runny mozzarella middles*

How to make baked potato mice

🥄 PREPARATION TIME **about 30 minutes**   🕐 COOKING TIME **about 1 hour**   🍽 SERVES 4

1 Preheat the oven to 400°F (200°C). Prick the potatoes with a fork. Brush them with oil. Bake for 1 hour, or until soft in the middle.

2 When cool enough to handle, cut off the tops and carefully scoop out the soft potato centers. You can throw away the lids (or eat them).

3 Mash the soft centers with butter, milk, and three-quarters of the cheese. Add salt and pepper. Put the mixture back into the potato skins.

Secure the nose with a toothpick.

4 Sprinkle with the remaining cheese. Broil the potatoes for 2–3 minutes, until golden.

5 Decorate each mouse with raisin eyes, a tomato nose, chive whiskers, radish ears, and a scallion tail.

Baked potato mice

Who could resist these gorgeous little baked potato mice? They're fun to make and even more fun to eat!

easy cheesy mice

How to make potato soufflés

🥘 PREPARATION **30 minutes** 🕐 COOKING TIME **about 17 minutes, plus cooking potatoes** 🍴 MAKES **4**

1 Preheat the oven to 425°F (220°C) and put a baking sheet in the oven to heat up. Then generously butter 4 ramekins.

2 Put the potato flesh in a bowl and mash well. Stir in the Parmesan and Cheddar cheeses, chives, and egg yolks.

3 Warm the milk and butter in a pan. Pour this over the potato mixture and stir well. Season with pepper (the Parmesan is already quite salty).

4 In a separate bowl, whisk the egg whites until they form light, soft peaks. Next, gently fold the egg whites into the potato mixture.

5 Fill the prepared ramekins with the mixture. Place them on the hot baking sheet and bake for 15–17 minutes, until puffed and golden.

Potato soufflés

The word soufflé comes from the French *souffler*, which means "to puff." When you see these come out of the oven, you'll understand why! Serve right away, so they don't have time to sink (although be careful, since they will be hot!).

You will need:

2 tbsp butter, plus extra for greasing
1 large baking potato, cooked
¼ cup grated Parmesan cheese
¾ cup grated sharp Cheddar cheese
small bunch chives, snipped into small pieces
2 eggs, separated
⅓ cup milk
pepper

☆Annabel's Tip
To cook the potato, either microwave it for 7–8 minutes, or boil it whole and unpeeled for 35 minutes, or until cooked.

How to make corn quesadillas

🥄 PREPARATION TIME **25 minutes**   🕐 COOKING TIME **about 8 minutes**   🍽 MAKES **4–5 quesadillas**

1 Chop up the red onion and the bell pepper. Drain the corn. Then grate the Cheddar cheese.

2 Heat the oil and stir-fry the onion and pepper for 3 minutes. Add the corn and cook for 2 minutes. Add the vinegar and honey. Cook for 1 minute.

3 Now spread the salsa over the middle of each tortilla. Top with the corn mixture.

4 Scatter a little cheese over the corn mixture. Save the rest for the top of each tortilla roll.

Preheat the broiler to high.

5 Roll up the tortillas and put them on a baking sheet. Scatter the remaining cheese on top. Broil for 1–2 minutes, until the cheese is lightly golden.

Corn quesadillas

Did you know that quesadillas (pronounced ke-sah-dee-uhs) are a Mexican dish? They are mildly spicy and make a super-tasty, super-popular meal.

You can use mild or medium salsa

You will need:

1 small red onion
½ red or orange bell pepper
1 cup drained, canned corn
4 oz (115 g) Cheddar cheese
1 tbsp olive oil
1 tbsp balsamic vinegar
1 tbsp honey
4 heaping tbsp salsa
4–5 flour or corn tortillas

How to make little pita pizzas

🥄 PREPARATION TIME **20 minutes**   🕐 COOKING TIME **1–2 minutes**   🍲 MAKES **4 mini pizzas**

1 For the tomato base, chop and fry the onion in oil for 5 minutes. Add the garlic and cook for 1 minute. Then stir in the tomato paste, ketchup, and 1 tbsp hot water.

2 Split the pitas in half and toast lightly, until crisp. Then spoon on the tomato base—spread it evenly across the pitas.

Toast until the cheese has melted.

3 Next, scatter the grated Cheddar cheese over the tomato base.

4 Choose your favorite toppings and place on top of the cheese. Try making a pattern or face. Toast the pitas for 1–2 minutes.

Little pita pizzas

Everyone loves pizza! So why not have a party where the guests can design their own pizza faces.

You will need:

1 small or ½ medium red onion
1 tbsp olive oil
1 small clove garlic, crushed
1 tbsp tomato paste
2 tsp ketchup
2 small round pitas or 1 large pita
½ cup grated Cheddar cheese
toppings of your choice (see below for ideas)

corn

ham

cherry tomatoes

bell peppers

How to make pasta salad

1 Cook the pasta following the package instructions. Rinse with cold water. Next, shred the chicken, slice the scallions, and deseed and chop the tomato.

2 Put the mayonnaise, yogurt, and lemon juice in a large bowl. Snip in the dill weed, season with salt and pepper, and then stir everything together.

3 Now add the cold pasta, chicken, scallions, chopped tomato, and corn to the mayonnaise mixture.

4 Mix all the ingredients together and spoon into colorful cups or bowls. Your pasta salad is now ready to eat.

Pasta salad

Corn, chicken, and noodles are often seen together in soups—and here I've used similar ingredients to make a yummy salad!

You will need:

8 oz (225 g) bow tie pasta
5½ oz (150 g) cooked chicken
4 scallions
1 large tomato
2 tbsp mayonnaise
2 tbsp Greek yogurt
½ tsp lemon juice
2-3 sprigs dill weed
salt and pepper
1 cup drained canned corn

☆Annabel's Tip
Pastas come in all shapes and sizes, including shells, twists (fusilli), and short tubes (penne). They all work well with this salad.

fresh crunchy salad

How to make spaghetti with tomato sauce

1 Heat the oil in a pan. Add the onion and garlic, and fry for 5 minutes, or until the onion is see-through and soft.

2 Add the canned tomatoes, tomato paste, balsamic vinegar, sugar, and salt and pepper. Cover with a lid and simmer for about 20 minutes.

3 In another pan, cook the spaghetti in boiling water. You can check the package to see how long you need to cook it.

4 Grate the Parmesan cheese, keeping your fingers safely away from the grater! Drain the pasta, put it into bowls, and top with the tomato sauce and grated cheese.

Spaghetti with tomato sauce

It's time to twirl the fork! This spaghetti dish makes healthy food fun. Serve it with tomato sauce to get your taste buds zinging.

Sprinkle with cheese and slurp away!

You will need:

2 tbsp olive oil
1 onion, peeled and chopped
1 clove garlic, crushed
14 oz (400 g) can diced
   tomatoes
½ tbsp tomato paste
½ tsp balsamic vinegar
½ tsp sugar
salt and pepper
7 oz (200 g) spaghetti
Parmesan cheese, to serve

How to make chicken and apple curry

🥘 PREPARATION TIME **10 minutes**   🕐 COOKING TIME **about 15 minutes**   🍽 SERVES **4**

Keep stirring constantly.

1 First, prepare the vegetables and fruit: peel and chop the onion, and crush the garlic. Then thinly slice the scallions and the apple.

2 Fry the onion in the oil for 5-6 minutes, until soft. Add the garlic and curry paste. Cook for 1 minute. Stir in the soy sauce, coconut milk, and stock.

3 Now add the lemongrass, chicken, and apple. Bring the curry to a boil, then simmer for 6-8 minutes, until the chicken is cooked through.

4 Add the peas and scallions, and cook for 1-2 minutes. Season to taste with salt and pepper (the soy sauce is salty too, so be careful).

Grease the molds with sunflower oil.

5 To shape the jasmine rice into star shapes, spoon the cooked rice into greased molds, press it down, then slip off the molds.

Chicken and apple curry

This mildly spicy curry is made with ingredients you can buy at your local supermarket. The apple adds a lovely sweetness to the dish.

Decorate with lime slices and cilantro

You will need:

1 onion
1 clove garlic
3 scallions
1 medium apple
1 tbsp vegetable oil
1-2 tsp mild curry paste
1 tsp soy sauce
⅔ cup coconut milk
1 chicken bouillon cube, dissolved in ⅔ cup boiling water
2 in (5 cm) piece lemongrass
2 chicken breasts, cubed
1 cup frozen peas
salt and pepper
boiled jasmine rice, sliced lime (2–3 slices), and cilantro (about 4–5 leaves), to serve

🥣 PREPARATION TIME **10 minutes, plus marinating** 🕐 COOKING TIME **45 minutes** 🍴 SERVES **2-4**

1 To prepare the marinade, first, pour the balsamic vinegar, soy sauce, and honey into a bowl.

2 Remove the papery skin from a clove of garlic and put the garlic in a garlic press. Then squeeze it into the bowl.

3 Peel a piece of fresh ginger and grate it into the bowl using a fine grater. It's easier if you freeze the ginger first.

4 Make cuts in the drumsticks and season with pepper. Put in an ovenproof dish. Pour the marinade over the chicken. Chill in the refrigerator for 20 minutes.

5 Preheat the oven to 400°F (200°C). Bake the drumsticks for 45 minutes, or until cooked through, turning and basting every 10 minutes.

Sticky chicken drumsticks

Pack this dish with taste and make it gorgeously sticky by soaking the drumsticks in a spicy-sweet marinade before cooking. This works the flavors into the meat and adds a lovely glaze.

Cook until golden brown

☆Annabel's Tip
If you are short on bowls, try marinating the chicken in a small plastic food bag.

How to make chicken satay

1 For the marinade, put the ginger, garlic, lime juice, soy sauce, peanut butter, and honey in a bowl and whisk together.

2 Put the chicken breasts in a sealable plastic bag. Pound them with a mallet until they are about ¼ in (5 mm) thick.

Finally, stir in the lime juice.

Turn over after 5 minutes.

3 Then slice each chicken breast into 5 strips and toss in the marinade. Leave for 10 minutes.

4 For the sauce, warm the peanut butter, coconut milk, water, chili sauce, and soy sauce, stirring until melted. Simmer for 1–2 minutes, until thickened.

5 Thread the chicken strips onto skewers and put on a foil-lined baking sheet. Broil for 10 minutes, until the chicken has cooked through.

Chicken satay

If you like peanut butter then you will enjoy this recipe. You can also make it with shrimp (two raw jumbo shrimp per skewer) or strips of beef.

☆Annabel's Tip
Soak the skewers in water for 30 minutes to stop them from going black when you broil them.

You will need:
2 chicken breasts

For the marinade
¼ tsp grated fresh ginger
1 clove garlic, crushed
juice of 1 lime
1 tbsp soy sauce
1 tsp peanut butter (creamy)
1 tbsp honey

For the satay sauce
½ cup peanut butter (crunchy)
5 tbsp coconut milk
5 tbsp water
1 tbsp sweet Thai chili sauce
1 tsp soy sauce
1 tsp lime juice

How to make sweet and sour pork

1 To make the sauce, heat the oil in a wok or a large frying pan. Stir-fry the onion and peppers for 4 minutes, or until they begin to soften.

2 Add the ginger and cook for 1 minute, then add the broth, soy sauce, sugar, vinegar, tomato paste, and canned pineapple with its juice.

Keep warm over low heat.

3 Bring to a boil and simmer for 1 minute. Add the cornstarch and simmer for 2–3 minutes, stirring until thickened. Keep warm.

4 Prepare the pork: whisk the egg yolk, cornstarch, salt, and milk together. Add the pork and mix until well coated.

Fry the pork in batches.

5 Heat the oil in a frying pan. Fry the pork over medium heat for 3–4 minutes, until it's golden on the outside and cooked through completely.

Sweet and sour pork

This delicious Chinese classic offers an exotic combination of very different flavors—sweet pineapple and sour vinegar.

TRY THIS WITH CHICKEN
This recipe works well with chicken, too. Simply swap the pork for 2 sliced chicken breasts.

You will need:

1 egg yolk
1½ tbsp cornstarch
pinch of salt
1 tbsp milk
8 oz (225 g) lean pork, cubed
2 tbsp canola oil

For the sauce
1 tbsp canola oil
1 red onion, roughly chopped
½ small red bell pepper, diced
½ small yellow bell pepper, diced
¼ tsp grated fresh ginger
½ cup chicken broth
1 tbsp soy sauce
½ tbsp light brown sugar
1 tbsp balsamic vinegar
1 tsp tomato paste
8 oz (227 g) can pineapple chunks
1 tbsp cornstarch mixed with 1 tbsp cold water

Mix the pork with the sauce and serve with rice

How to make lamb tagine

🍲 PREPARATION TIME **20 minutes**   🕐 COOKING TIME **2½ to 3 hours**   🍽 SERVES **4–6**

1 Mix the flour with ¼ tsp salt and a grinding of black pepper. Toss the lamb in the seasoned flour to coat it.

2 Heat 1 tbsp of the oil in a frying pan and brown the lamb—you may need to do this in batches. Put the browned lamb aside.

3 Heat 1 tbsp oil in a deep pan. Add the onion and cook until soft. Stir in the garlic, cinnamon, cumin, and curry powder, and cook for 2 minutes.

4 Stir in the broth, tomatoes, paste, honey, apple, and lamb. Bring to a boil. Reduce heat to low, cover, and cook for 1½–2 hours, stirring occasionally.

Add broth a little at a time.

5 Uncover and stir in the apricots. Simmer for 30 minutes. Add ¼ cup extra water if the sauce is too thick. Add the salt and pepper.

Lamb tagine

Try my special version of a traditional Moroccan recipe. It's meaty, spicy, and fruity all at once! Serve it with couscous.

Garnish with fresh cilantro

You will need:

2 tbsp all-purpose flour
salt and pepper
1 lb (450 g) diced lamb
2 to 3 tbsp canola oil
1 onion, chopped
1 clove garlic, crushed
½ tsp cinnamon
½ tsp cumin
2 tsp mild curry powder
1¼ cups vegetable broth
14 oz (400 g) can tomatoes
3 tbsp tomato paste
1 tsp honey
½ apple, grated
¾ cup quartered dried apricots

☆Annabel's Tip
This dish freezes well, so make twice the amount you need and freeze some for another day.

How to make the best hamburgers

1 First, peel and chop the onion into small pieces. Heat the oil and gently cook the onion for 8 minutes or until it's soft. Stir in the sugar and balsamic vinegar.

2 Turn up the heat and cook, stirring, for 2 minutes, until the onion caramelizes (the sugar on it turns light brown). Add the thyme. Put the mixture in a bowl to cool.

3 Add the beef, bread crumbs, egg yolk, milk, soy sauce, and salt and pepper. Mix everything together lightly so the burgers stay soft and moist when they cook.

4 Divide the mixture into four and roll into four balls. Flatten these slightly. Cover and chill in the refrigerator.

Shape into hamburgers

5 Lightly grease a frying pan. Cook the burgers over low heat for 4 to 5 minutes on each side. Alternatively, broil for about 4 minutes on each side.

Best hamburgers

These juicy burgers are made from lean ground beef flavored with caramelized onion, thyme, and soy sauce. They're delicious fried in a little oil, but if you want to cut down on fat, try broiling them instead.

You will need:

1 red onion
1 tbsp olive oil
4 tsp light brown sugar
1 tbsp balsamic vinegar
4 sprigs thyme
7 oz (200 g) lean ground beef
¾ cup fresh bread crumbs
1 egg yolk
2 tbsp milk
1 tsp soy sauce
salt and pepper
sunflower oil, for frying

☆Annabel's Tip
Serve each hamburger in a bun, along with a few lettuce leaves, sliced tomato and red onion, and a little mayonnaise.

How to make risotto primavera

1 Dice the carrot, then thinly slice the leek and the onion. Now crush the garlic and dice the zucchini.

2 Melt the butter in a large saucepan. Add the oil, then sauté the onion gently for 4 minutes, until softened. Add the leek, carrot, and garlic and sauté until the leek has softened.

3 Add the rice and cook for 1 minute, then stir in a ladleful of stock and cook slowly until the liquid is absorbed, stirring all the time.

Stir regularly while cooking.

4 Add the rest of the stock one ladleful at a time—wait for it to be absorbed before adding more. After about 18 minutes it will be almost cooked through.

Season with pepper and serve.

5 Add the zucchini and peas. Cook for about 4 minutes, until the vegetables are cooked through. Remove from the heat and stir in the grated cheese.

Risotto primavera

This Italian classic is a super-tasty, meat-free, meal in a bowl. It's made with meltingly soft rice, summer vegetables, and Parmesan cheese.

Scatter cheese shavings on top before serving

You will need:

1 small carrot
1 small leek
1 small onion
1 small clove garlic
½ medium zucchini
1 tbsp butter
1 tbsp olive oil
1 cup risotto rice
5 cups hot vegetable stock
¾ cup frozen peas
½ cup grated Parmesan cheese, plus shavings to serve
freshly ground black pepper

☆Annabel's Tip

For perfect risotto, the rice should be al dente. This means soft but not mushy—when you bite in, it should still be a little firm.

How to make paella

PREPARATION TIME **about 10 minutes**   ⏱ COOKING TIME **30 minutes**   🍽 SERVES **4**

1 First, finely chop the onion, dice the pepper, and crush the garlic. Then heat the oil in a large nonstick frying pan and cook the onion, stirring, for 5 minutes until soft.

2 Add the pepper, garlic, and paprika. Pour in the rice and cook everything for 3 minutes, stirring constantly.

Add water if the rice looks dry.

3 Mix the broth and tomato paste in a bowl. Pour this onto the rice mixture. Simmer for 15 minutes, until the rice is tender and the broth is absorbed.

4 While the rice is cooking, shred the chicken into small pieces and roughly chop the parsley leaves.

5 Pour the peas, shrimp, and chicken into the paella and cook for another 2 minutes. Scatter the chopped parsley over the top and serve.

Paella

Paella was first made in Spain and gets its name from the pan in which it was cooked—a *paellera*. This is a *paella mixta*, using seafood and chicken.

You will need:

1 onion
½ red bell pepper
1 clove garlic
1 tbsp olive oil
1 tsp smoked paprika or
  sweet paprika
1 cup long-grain rice
2½ cups chicken broth
2 tbsp tomato paste
6 oz (175 g) cooked chicken
handful parsley leaves
½ cup frozen peas
6 oz (175 g) cooked, peeled
  shrimp

☆ **Annabel's Tip**
Use this recipe to make an even more tomato-ey paella. Simply reduce the stock to 1 cup and add a 14 oz (400 g) can of chopped tomatoes at step 3.

Honey-glazed salmon

Here I've used honey and soy sauce to make a glaze called teriyaki. It's delicious on salmon.

You will need:

¼ cup honey
4 tsp soy sauce
2 tsp rice wine vinegar
¼ tsp grated fresh ginger
6 oz (175 g) skinless salmon
  fillet, cut into cubes
1 tsp water

☆ Annabel's Tip

Before you begin, soak the wooden skewers in warm water for 30 minutes.

🍲 PREPARATION TIME **10 minutes**   ⏱ COOKING TIME **30 minutes**   🍴 SERVES **2-4**

Mix and coat the salmon well.

1 Mix the honey, soy sauce, and vinegar together. Set half aside in a pan. Add ginger to the remaining mixture and pour onto the salmon.

2 Thread the salmon onto the skewers. Put them on a foil-lined baking sheet. Spoon on the sauce from the bowl.

Broil under high heat.

3 Broil the salmon for 2–3 minutes on each side. Add the water to the sauce in the pan. Simmer for 30 seconds. Serve with the salmon.

MAIN MEALS

Salmon fishcakes

These delicious little fishcakes will be swimming off your plate in no time!

☆Annabel's Tip

While the fishcakes cool, mix the dip ingredients together in a small bowl.

You will need:

7½ oz (212 g) can pink salmon, drained and mashed
2 scallions, chopped
2 tsp lemon juice
½ tbsp mayonnaise
½ tbsp ketchup
¾ cup fresh bread crumbs
2 tbsp all-purpose flour
⅓ cup dry bread crumbs
1 egg, beaten
2 tbsp canola oil
frozen peas, cooked (3–6)

For the dip
2 tbsp mayonnaise
1 tsp lemon juice
1 tsp Thai sweet chili sauce

🍽 PREPARATION TIME **25 minutes**   ⏱ COOKING TIME **about 3 minutes each**   🍽 MAKES 6

Shape a few patties like a fish.

1 Mix together the salmon, onions, juice, mayonnaise, ketchup, and fresh bread crumbs. Divide the mixture into 6 balls and shape into rounds or fish.

2 Put the flour, dry bread crumbs, and beaten egg on separate plates. Dip each fishcake in flour, then egg, and then bread crumbs.

Add a pea for each eye.

3 Make an eye on the fish-shaped fishcakes. Then fry the fishcakes in the oil for 1½ minutes on each side, until golden.

How to make salmon in pastry

1 Melt the butter and sauté the shallot or onion for 8–10 minutes, or until softened. Transfer to a bowl to cool.

2 Squeeze out the moisture from the spinach. Then chop it and add it to the onion, along with the ricotta, Parmesan, and nutmeg. Add salt and pepper.

3 Cut each pastry sheet in half. Then roll each piece to a rectangle about 6 in x 16 in (15 cm x 40 cm).

Trim to make a fish shape.

4 Place a portion of salmon on the pastry and top with the spinach mixture. Brush a little beaten egg around the salmon and fold the pastry over.

5 Brush with beaten egg and chill for 1 hour. Preheat the oven to 400°F (200°C). Brush with the egg again. Bake on a baking sheet for 25 minutes.

Make a face with pastry scraps.

Salmon in pastry

These little salmon parcels make perfect picnic food. I've shaped mine into pastry fish, but simple rectangular parcels are just as much fun to eat.

Salmon inside

You will need:

1 tbsp butter
1 large shallot or 1 small onion, diced
4½ oz (125 g) baby spinach, cooked and drained
½ cup ricotta cheese
¼ cup grated Parmesan cheese
pinch of grated nutmeg
salt and pepper
2 sheets ready-rolled puff pastry from a 17.3 oz (490 g) package
10 oz (300 g) salmon fillet, divided into 4 equal portions
1 egg, beaten

How to make fish parcels

PREPARATION TIME **about 10 minutes**   COOKING TIME **about 20 minutes**   SERVES 2

Season with salt and pepper.

1 Preheat the oven to 400°F (200°C). Sauté the shallot in butter until soft. Add the tomatoes, tomato paste, stock, and juice. Simmer for 3 minutes. Stir in the sugar, basil, and olives.

2 Grease 2 squares of parchment paper or foil, about 12 in (30 cm). Place a piece of fish on each square and season with salt and pepper.

A fish parcel

looks like this

3 Spoon the tomato sauce on the fish and wrap up the parchment paper like a package, folding over the edges to seal them.

4 Finally, place the parcels on a baking sheet and bake for 12 to 14 minutes, or until the fish is cooked through.

Fish parcels

Wouldn't you love to open a steaming parcel at dinnertime? Cooking fish in parchment paper or foil is a delicious way to seal in its goodness—and there are no fishy smells!

☆Annabel's Tip

Make sure you seal your parcels well—if there's a hole where steam can escape, your fish may dry out.

You will need:

oil, for greasing
2 skinless, boneless, thick
  white fish fillets (such as
  cod or haddock)
salt and pepper

For the tomato sauce
1 small shallot, finely chopped
1 tbsp butter
4 tomatoes, skinned, deseeded
  and chopped
2 tsp tomato paste
2 tbsp fish or vegetable stock
½ tsp lemon juice
pinch of sugar
4 basil leaves, shredded
black olives, sliced

How to make fruit smoothies

🍲 PREPARATION TIME **about 10 minutes each**   🍽️ SERVES **2 each**

Summertime smoothie

1 banana
4 large strawberries
2 peaches
½ cup vanilla yogurt
½ cup orange juice

Coconut dream

½ cup coconut milk
1¼ cups pineapple juice
2 scoops vanilla ice cream
4 oz (115 g) fresh pineapple, diced
mint, to serve (optional)

Peach melba

1 cup raspberries
3 large peaches, peeled, pitted and sliced
1 cup raspberry drinking yogurt

1 Cut a few slices from the banana and strawberries and put the rest into a blender. Peel the peaches and put the flesh into the blender, too.

1 Put the coconut milk, pineapple juice, vanilla ice cream, and pineapple (keep aside two pieces) in a blender and process.

1 Get rid of any seeds by pressing the raspberries through a strainer.

2 Add the yogurt and orange juice to the fruit, and blend until smooth. Push the strawberry and banana slices onto straws and serve.

2 Pour the drink into glasses. Decorate with pineapple pieces and mint, if using, then serve.

2 Blend the raspberries, peach (except two slices), and yogurt. Pour into glasses, decorate with the peach slices, and serve.

Fruit smoothies

Fruit is not only juicy and scrumptious, but it also keeps you healthy and helps you grow strong! Here I've used fruit to make three delicious smoothies. All you have to do is combine a few ingredients in a blender.

coconut dream

peach melba

summertime smoothie

How to make my favorite crepes

1 Sift the flour and salt together into a mixing bowl. Then make a well in the center of the flour.

2 Break the eggs into the well. Whisk the eggs and flour together. Now mix the water and milk together in a separate bowl or pitcher.

3 Add the liquid to the flour, a little at a time, whisking to make a smooth batter. Melt 2 tbsp of the butter and stir it into the batter. Strain if lumpy.

4 Melt a little butter in a frying pan. Add the batter—about 2 tbsp per crepe. Spread the batter to cover the pan.

5 Cook the crepe for about 1 minute. Use a spatula to loosen it, then flip it over! Cook the second side for 30 seconds.

My favorite crepes

A foolproof crepe batter—no flops when you flip these! Keep the crepes thin so they come out nice and light and crispy.

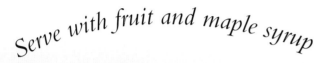

Serve with fruit and maple syrup

You will need:

1 cup all-purpose flour
a pinch of salt
2 eggs
¼ cup water
1 cup milk
¼ cup (½ stick) butter

for the filling:
fresh berries such as
   strawberries, blueberries,
   and raspberries
2 tbsp maple syrup

How to make fruit kebabs and mango dip

🥣 PREPARATION TIME **20 minutes**   🍽 SERVES **2–4**

1 First, cut up the mango—one way is to slice it in half and remove the pit. Then cut the flesh into cubes. Turn the skin inside out. Cut off the cubes.

2 Use a fork or potato masher to mash the mango into a smooth pulp.

3 Stir in the Greek yogurt and honey to sweeten.

4 To make the fruity kebabs, simply thread your cubed fruit onto skewers.

5 Decorate the dip (if you want to) and serve with the fruit kebabs.

Get dipping!

Fruit kebabs with mango dip

These colorful kebabs make a perfect dessert or light snack. You can use almost any fruit to make them, then start dipping!

You will need:

For the dip
1 mango (or use peach instead)
⅔ cup Greek yogurt
1 tsp honey

For the skewers
selection of your favorite fruit, cubed

Nectarine

Pineapple

Grape

Melon

Strawberry

☆Annabel's Tip
It's fun to decorate the dip for younger children. I've made mine look like a fish, using slices of fruit and a chocolate chip for the eye.

How to make banana bites

PREPARATION TIME **about 30 minutes**   MAKES **about 6**

1 Peel the banana and trim off the ends. Chop the flesh into about 6 pieces.

2 Break the chocolate into a heatproof bowl. Put the bowl over a pan of simmering water and melt the chocolate, stirring occasionally. Leave to cool slightly.

3 Push a straw through each piece of the banana, then drizzle the melted chocolate over it.

4 Roll the chocolate-covered banana in the coconut or sprinkles. Let the chocolate harden, then serve.

Banana bites

This light dessert is fun for children to make (it can be a little messy!). It works best with slightly underripe bananas.

You will need:

1–2 bananas
4 oz (115 g) chocolate—
  milk or semi-sweet
shredded coconut
sprinkles

☆Annabel's Tip
Strawberries are also delicious with chocolate. Simply hold them by the stalk, dip in melted chocolate, and eat!

coconut

chocolate sprinkles

colored sprinkles

How to make fruit brûlée

🥄 PREPARATION TIME **20 minutes, plus chilling**   🕐 COOKING TIME **about 5 minutes**   🍽️ SERVES **4**

1 Hull and quarter the strawberries and put them into a bowl with the blueberries. Dust 1 tbsp of the confectioners' sugar over the top and toss to coat the berries.

2 Whisk the cream to soft peaks. In a separate bowl, mix together the yogurt, vanilla, and remaining confectioners' sugar. Now fold the cream into the yogurt.

3 Spoon the berries into 4 custard cups and put the yogurt mixture on top.

4 Sprinkle on the Demerara sugar, then place the brûlées in the freezer for 15 minutes. Heat the broiler to high. Broil as close as possible to the heat until the sugar has melted.

Fruit brûlée

Yogurt makes a perfect topping for a fruit brûlée. Brûlée means "burned" in French, but really the sugar topping is broiled until it has just melted and caramelized.

Cool before serving so the crust becomes crispy

You will need:

7 oz (200 g) strawberries
1 cup blueberries
3 tbsp confectioners' sugar
⅔ cup heavy cream
7 oz (200 g) Greek yogurt
½ tsp vanilla extract
2 tbsp Demerara sugar

How to make easy berry ice cream

1 Wash all the berries—pick out any bits of stalk—and hull the strawberries.

2 Put the berries and the superfine sugar in a pan, cover, and cook slowly for 5 to 10 minutes.

3 When the berries let out their juices, turn up the heat and simmer for 5 minutes.

4 Let the fruits cool, then blend them until smooth.

5 Now strain the blended fruits to remove the seeds.

6 Pour the strained fruit into ice cube trays and freeze until solid.

7 Put the cream in a bowl and whip it until it forms soft peaks.

8 Take the berries out of the freezer and thaw for 5 minutes, then roughly chop in a blender. Add the cream.

9 Blend to combine, then add confectioners' sugar to taste. Serve immediately, or freeze for an hour before serving.

Easy berry ice cream

This fresh, fruity ice cream is packed with berries. And you don't need an ice cream machine to make it!

How to make raspberry ripple cheesecake

1 Put the crackers in a bag. Then use a rolling pin to crush them into crumbs. Melt the butter in a pan and pour the crackers into it. Stir thoroughly.

2 Line an 8 in (20 cm) cake pan (with a removeable bottom) with plastic wrap. Spoon in the cracker mixture, press it flat, and put it in the refrigerator.

3 Simmer the raspberries and confectioners' sugar for 3 minutes, then strain. Mix the cornstarch with 2 tsp cold water. Stir into the raspberry puree. Simmer until thick.

Top with the remaining cheese mixture. Use the remaining puree to decorate the top.

4 As the raspberry puree cools, beat together the cream cheese, superfine sugar, and vanilla. Whip the cream until stiff, then fold it into the cheese mixture.

5 Spread ⅔ of the cheese mixture on the crumb crust. Swirl in ⅔ of the raspberry puree.

Raspberry ripple cheesecake

Swirl raspberries and cream together to make the dreamiest cheesecake ever! Chill before serving.

You will need:

9 oz (250 g) graham crackers (about 18 crackers)
½ cup (1 stick) plus 1 tbsp butter
2½ cups fresh raspberries
½ cup confectioners' sugar
1 tsp cornstarch
1 lb (450 g) cream cheese
1 cup superfine sugar
1 tsp vanilla extract
1¾ cup heavy cream

Raspberry topping
For a feathered effect, drizzle on parallel lines of the remaining raspberry puree and pull a skewer across these lines.

Leave the cheesecake in the refrigerator for at least 2 hours

How to make mini lemon cheesecakes

🍮 **PREPARATION TIME** 45 minutes, plus chilling   🍽 **SERVES 4**

Oil the insides of the rings.

1 First, put the crackers in a plastic bag and crush them using a rolling pin. Then melt the butter in a saucepan and stir in the cracker crumbs.

2 Divide the crumb mixture into a selection of ring molds. Press firmly into each crust. Chill in the refrigerator while you make the topping.

3 Mix together the yogurt, lemon curd, and lemon juice in a large bowl, until smooth. In another bowl, whip the cream until it forms soft peaks.

4 Mix 2 tbsp of the whipped cream into the lemon and yogurt mixture. Then fold in the remaining cream.

5 Spoon the lemon mixture on top of the chilled crumb crusts. Smooth off with a metal spatula. Chill before serving.

Mini lemon cheesecakes

These sweet, little cheesecakes are so deliciously lemony, you might want to make double quantities!

Top with berries and confectioners' sugar

☆Annabel's Tip
To remove the cheesecakes from the rings, run a knife around the inside edge, then lift off the rings.

Baked apples

Dessert or cooking apples are equally good in this super-simple recipe. It's delicious when served with a lovely big topping of yogurt!

You will need:

4 apples
⅓ cup raisins
3 tbsp light brown sugar
¼ tsp cinnamon
1 tbsp butter
⅓ cup water

☆ Annabel's Tip
Before cooking, score around the apples so they don't burst open.

🍏 PREPARATION TIME **10 minutes**　　　🕐 COOKING TIME **about 40 minutes**　　　🍽 SERVES **4**

1 Preheat the oven to 350°F (180°C). Remove the cores from the apples using an apple corer. Then put the apples in a baking dish.

2 Mix together the raisins, light brown sugar, and cinnamon. Stuff this mixture into the holes in the apples. Top with the butter.

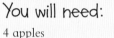

3 Pour about ⅓ cup water around the apples so it just covers the bottom of the dish. Bake for 35–40 minutes, basting halfway through cooking.

Apple meringue tarts

These simple little apple tarts topped with meringue are delicious warm or cold. Serve them with vanilla yogurt or cream.

You will need:

For the tarts
7 oz (200 g) ready-rolled
  pie crust
2-3 apples, peeled and chopped
2 tbsp water
1 tbsp superfine sugar
1 tsp lemon juice

For the meringue
1 large egg white
3 tbsp superfine sugar

🥣 PREPARATION TIME **20 minutes**   🕐 COOKING TIME **about 20 minutes**   🍽 SERVES **6**

Bake for 15 minutes.

1 ⚠ Preheat the oven to 400°F (200°C). Cut 6 circles from the pie crust. Line a muffin pan with the pie crust circles.

2 ⚠ Cook the apples in the water until soft. Stir in the sugar and juice. Let the apples cool, then mash them. Spoon into the pie crust shells.

3 ⚠ For the meringue, whisk the egg white to stiff peaks. Add the sugar, 1 tbsp at a time. Pipe or spoon onto the apple pies and bake for another 3-5 minutes.

How to make traffic light ice pops

🍅 PREPARATION TIME **30 minutes, plus freezing**   🍽️ MAKES 2–4

Freeze for 1½ hours.

Freeze again until solid.

Add the sticks and freeze.

1 For the red, remove the melon seeds. Puree the flesh with 2 tbsp of the sugar in a blender. Pour into ice pop molds so they are all ⅓ full.

2 For the yellow, blend the peaches with 2 tbsp of the sugar. Pour onto the frozen red puree so the molds are now ⅔ full.

3 For the green, blend the kiwi fruit with the water and 2 tbsp sugar. Strain the puree to remove the seeds. Fill the ice pop molds.

How to make berry ice pops

🍅 PREPARATION TIME **10 minutes, plus freezing**   🕐 COOKING TIME **about 5 minutes**   🍽️ MAKES 2–4

1 Boil the sugar and water in a pan. Stir constantly until the sugar has dissolved.

2 Puree, then strain the strawberries and raspberries. Mix with the orange juice and sugary water.

3 Pour the mixture into ice pop molds. Put in the sticks and freeze until solid.

Fresh fruit ice pops

You'll need a blender to make these ice pops. Just check that they are completely frozen before you eat them—and enjoy!

Berry ice pop

Traffic light ice pop

You will need:

For traffic light ice pops
½ small watermelon
⅓ cup superfine sugar
3 large ripe peaches, peeled
5 large ripe kiwi fruit, peeled
3 tbsp water

For berry ice pops
3 tbsp superfine sugar
¼ cup water
1¼ cups sliced strawberries
1¼ cups raspberries
juice of 2 medium oranges

Fruit skewers

Make traffic light fruit skewers with scoops of different colored melons.

You will need:

1 watermelon (red)
1 cantaloupe (orange)
1 honeydew melon (green)

☆ Annabel's Tip
You can also add these melon balls to bowls of ice cream for a tasty, hot weather treat.

🥣 PREPARATION TIME **20 minutes**   🍽 SERVES 8–10

1 Cut the melons in half and use a melon scoop to make balls of different colors.

2 Push a straw through the middle of the balls of melon. On each straw, put red at the top, then orange, then green.

Homemade lemonade

This is a refreshing drink for a hot day and is packed with vitamin C!

You will need:

1 cup sugar
⅔ cup boiled water
6 large lemons
3¾ cups chilled still
  or sparkling water

☆Annabel's Tip
Serve with mint leaves and slices of lemon.

🥣PREPARATION TIME **20 minutes**   🍽MAKES **5 cups**

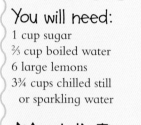

1 Mix the sugar and hot water in a heatproof bowl. Stir to dissolve the sugar, then set aside to cool. Roll the lemons to release the juice.

2 Squeeze the lemons. You need about 1 cup of the lemon juice.

3 Pour the juice into a pitcher and stir in the sugar syrup. Finally, add the chilled water and mix.

How to make chocolate orange brownies

1 Preheat the oven to 350°F (180°C). Line an 8 in (20 cm) square cake pan with parchment paper.

2 Put the butter, sugar, and dark chocolate in a large heatproof bowl. Set it over a saucepan of simmering water.

3 Let the butter and chocolate melt, stirring occasionally. Remove the bowl from the saucepan and leave to cool.

4 Prepare the orange zest and juice. Then whisk these together with the eggs, vanilla, and salt, until combined.

5 Whisk the orange and egg mixture into the cooled melted chocolate.

6 Sift the flour, cocoa powder, and baking powder onto the chocolate mixture and fold it in.

7 Now add the white chocolate chips and fold these in, too.

8 Pour into the prepared pan. Bake for 30 minutes if you want fudgelike brownies or for 35 minutes for cakelike brownies.

9 When done, let the brownies cool completely in the pan before removing them. Cut into squares and serve.

Chocolate orange brownies

Bake a batch of rich brownies for a special treat. Decide whether you like them fudgelike or cakelike, and adjust the cooking time to suit.

You will need:

- 1 cup (2 sticks) butter
- 1¼ cups light brown sugar
- 7 oz (200 g) semi-sweet chocolate
- zest of 1 large orange
- juice of ½ orange
- 4 eggs
- 1 tsp vanilla extract
- large pinch of salt
- 1 cup all-purpose flour
- ¼ cup unsweetened cocoa powder
- 1 tsp baking powder
- 4 oz (115 g) chopped white chocolate or ½ cup chocolate chips

How to make marble cake

🥣 PREPARATION **25 minutes**   🕐 COOKING TIME **about 1 hour**   🍽 SERVES 8

1 Preheat the oven to 350°F (180°C). Grease a Bundt pan 8½ in (21½ cm) across and 4 in (10 cm) deep.

2 Melt the chocolate in a bowl set over a pan of simmering water. Then set it aside to cool.

3 Cream the butter and sugar until light and fluffy.

4 Beat in the eggs, a little at a time. If the mixture curdles (separates), add 1 tbsp of flour and continue beating.

5 Then sift the flour and salt over this mixture. Fold this in, then add the sour cream and fold this in, too.

6 Divide the mixture equally between two bowls. Stir the vanilla extract into one of the bowls of mixture.

7 Add the cocoa powder and the melted chocolate to the other bowl. Stir to combine.

Swirl to get the marble effect.

8 Put alternating spoonfuls of chocolate and vanilla in the pan. Bake for 50–55 minutes, or until the cake is risen and firm.

9 Cool in the pan for 20 minutes. Then turn out onto a wire rack and leave to cool completely before frosting.

Marble cake

Inside this cake are swirls of chocolate and vanilla. These are made from the same basic cake mixture, but have different flavorings.

You will need:

1¾ cups (3 ½ sticks) unsalted butter, plus extra for greasing
3 oz (85 g) semi-sweet chocolate
1¼ cups superfine sugar
4 eggs, lightly beaten
1¾ cups self-rising flour
large pinch of salt
2 tbsp sour cream
1 tsp vanilla extract
1½ tbsp unsweetened cocoa powder

Chocolate frosting

Put 3 oz (85 g) semi-sweet chocolate, 3 tbsp milk, and 2 tbsp light corn syrup into a heatproof bowl set over a pan of hot water. Leave to melt, stirring occasionally. Then cool the frosting slightly and drizzle it over the cake.

How to make banana butterfly cupcakes

1 Preheat the oven to 350°F (180°C). Line a muffin pan with 8 muffin cups. Peel and mash the banana. Set it aside.

2 Beat the butter and sugar in a large bowl until pale and fluffy. In a separate bowl, whisk the eggs and vanilla. Add the eggs to the butter mixture, a little at a time, beating thoroughly.

3 Now add the banana to the butter mixture and stir it in. Then sift the flour over the top and fold this in.

4 Fill the muffin cups with the mixture. Bake for 20 minutes, or until risen and springy to the touch.

5 For the frosting, beat together the cream cheese and butter. Add the Dulche de Leche and confectioners' sugar.

Banana butterfly cupcakes

These little cupcakes can be eaten plain or covered in my sweet and sticky caramel topping—they'll be a flyaway success!

☆Annabel's Tip

To make butterfly wings, slice off the tops of the cupcakes. Cut them in half, dust with confectioners' sugar, and draw on the wings with writing icing. Pipe on the frosting and add the wings on top.

You will need:

For the cupcakes
1 large banana
½ cup (1 stick) butter
½ cup superfine sugar
2 eggs
¾ tsp vanilla extract
1 cup self-rising flour

For the caramel frosting
3 oz (85 g) cream cheese
3 tbsp unsalted butter
3 oz (85 g) Dulche de Leche
¼ cup confectioners' sugar, plus extra for dusting

How to make a cupcake farm

🥄 PREPARATION **50 minutes**   🕐 COOKING TIME **18–20 minutes**   🍴 MAKES **12 cupcakes**

Beat until smooth and light.

1 Preheat the oven to 350°F (180°C). Beat together the eggs, vanilla, superfine sugar, margarine, and flour.

2 Line a muffin pan with paper muffin cups, and half fill each cup with the cupcake mixture.

3 Bake for 18–20 minutes. When done, the cupcakes will rise up, turn golden in color, and spring back when pressed.

Add food coloring for pink frosting.

4 For the frosting, beat the butter until creamy. Slowly beat in the confectioners' sugar. Then beat in the water.

5 To make the marshmallow sheep, spread a thick layer of butter frosting over the top of the cupcakes.

6 Stick on marshmallows—large for heads, halved for ears, and mini ones for woolly coats. Use writing icing for glue.

7 For the piggy cupcakes, stick on a nose made from a large marshmallow and ears made from slices of marshmallow.

8 For puppy cupcakes, stick cookie ears on frosting. Use chocolate chips or candy-coated chocolates for eyes and noses.

9 Draw the faces on your animals using writing icing squeezed from a tube.

Cupcake farm

Make your own cupcakes, then turn them into sheep, pigs, and puppies. They really are the sweetest animals on the farm!

Puppy cupcakes

Piggy cupcakes

How to make animal cookies

1 Preheat the oven to 350°F (180°C). Beat together the butter, sugar, egg, and vanilla extract in a large bowl. Sift in the flour and salt. Mix again to make the dough.

2 Now it is time to get sticky! Press the dough together with your hands to make a ball.

3 Roll the dough between a folded piece of parchment paper until it's about ¼ in (5 mm) thick.

4 Cut out shapes from the dough using cookie cutters. Gather the trimmings into a ball, then roll out again and cut more shapes.

Decorate the cookies when they are cool.

5 Lift the cookies with a metal spatula and arrange them slightly apart on nonstick baking sheets. Bake for 14 minutes. Cool on a wire rack.

Animal cookies

It's fun to roll out dough and cut it into shapes, especially when it's for making cookies. So dig out your cookie cutters and get started!

Decorate using writing icing

You will need:

1 cup plus 2 tbsp (2¼ sticks)
   butter (room temperature)
⅔ cup superfine sugar
1 egg yolk
2 tsp vanilla extract
   2¾ cups all-purpose flour
   ¼ tsp salt

☆Annabel's Tip
To make chocolate cookies, split the dough into two at step 2 and add 1 tbsp unsweetened cocoa powder to one half.

How to make chocolate fridge cake

🥄 PREPARATION TIME **30 minutes, plus chilling**   🍽 MAKES **12–24 slices**

1 Put the graham crackers in a plastic bag and crush them into pieces with a rolling pin.

2 Melt both kinds of chocolate, the butter, and light corn syrup in a heatproof bowl set over a pan of hot water. Stir well.

3 Remove the bowl from the heat and stir in the broken graham crackers, apricots, raisins, and pecans (optional).

4 Line an 8 in (20 cm) shallow, square-shaped pan with plastic wrap. Spoon the mix into the pan. Level it by pressing down with a potato masher.

Cut into slices and serve.

5 Set the cake in the fridge for 1–2 hours. Then turn it out and peel off the plastic wrap.

Chocolate fridge cake

This no-bake cake keeps fresh in the fridge for two weeks (if it lasts that long!).

You will need:

9 oz (250 g) graham crackers
5 oz (140 g) semi-sweet chocolate
5 oz (140 g) milk chocolate
½ cup (1 stick) unsalted butter
⅔ cup light corn syrup
⅔ cup dried apricots, chopped
½ cup raisins
½ cup chopped pecans, (optional)

☆Annabel's Tip

This cake is incredibly rich, so only have a little at a time.

Peanut butter bears

It just takes a little mixing and shaping to make these crispy bear heads.

You will need:

¾ cup puffed rice cereal
½ cup confectioners' sugar
2 tbsp sesame seeds
½ cup smooth peanut butter
3 tbsp unsalted butter

To decorate
16 chocolate chips
candy-coated chocolates
black writing icing

PREPARATION TIME 30 minutes, plus chilling   **MAKES 8 bears**

Slightly flatten each ball.

Chill for 30 minutes, then serve.

1 Mix together the puffed rice cereal, confectioners' sugar, and sesame seeds. Melt the peanut butter and butter in a pan and add to the mixture.

2 Divide the mixture into 8 parts (roughly 2 tbsp each) and roll into balls. Put the balls on a baking sheet lined with parchment paper.

3 Create bear faces. Make ears with chocolate chips and push in candy-coated chocolates for eyes and noses. Use writing icing to draw on mouths.